THE JOY OF LEARNING

The Joy of Learning

INSPIRING CURIOSITY IN CHILDREN

Avery Nightingale

Creative Quill Press

Contents

1

Chapter 1: Introduction to the Joy of Learning

The Flash of Interest

At the core of each and every revelation, each development, and each imaginative undertaking lies a straightforward, yet significant flash: interest. This normal craving to comprehend, to investigate, and to realize drives humankind forward. Also, it is inside the early long stretches of experience growing up that this flash consumes most brilliantly. Encouraging an affection for learning in youngsters isn't just about setting them up for school; it's tied in with setting the establishment for a satisfying, drew in, and inquisitive life.

Significance of Encouraging an Affection for Learning in Youngsters

An adoration for learning is quite possibly of the most valuable gift we can provide for the future. The key makes the way for a long period of chances, revelations, and development. At the point when kids are urged to investigate their inclinations, get clarification on pressing issues, and look for replies, they foster a feeling of trust in their capacity to grasp the world. This upgrades their scholastic presentation as well as supports their close to home and social turn of events.

Figuring out how to cherish learning implies youngsters will be more versatile in a quickly impacting world. They will be issue solvers, scholars who look past the surface, and people who look for consistent improvement in themselves and their environmental elements. Also, this affection for learning develops flexibility, permitting kids to confront difficulties and disappointments as vital stages in the educational experience.

Outline of the Advantages of Long lasting Learning

Long lasting learning expands the delight and advantages of this mission for information a long ways past the study hall. It envelops self-improvement, professional success, and the sheer delight of revelation. Deep rooted students are more versatile to changes in the gig market, are more imaginative, and will generally have really fulfilling and better existences.

The advantages of long lasting learning include:

•Improved mental capability and memory maintenance.

•Expanded sympathy and grasping through the investigation of different societies and points of view.

•Worked on close to home wellbeing and stress the board abilities.

•The ceaseless transformation of abilities and information to explore the advancing requests of the expert world.

Making way for Interest and Investigation

Establishing a climate that energizes interest and investigation is significant. It includes something other than giving data; it's tied in with moving kids to inquire, "Why?" "How?" and "Imagine a scenario in which?" This climate energizes active encounters, decisive reasoning, and critical thinking. It esteems the most common way of advancing as much as the result, encouraging a feeling of bliss and marvel despite the unexplored world.

Guardians, instructors, and parental figures can set this stage by:

•Empowering inquiries without a right or wrong answer and esteeming all requests.

•Giving assorted encounters and assets to animate interest and disclosure.

•Demonstrating an adoration for learning and interest in their own lives.

•Offering strong criticism and praising endeavors, not simply accomplishments.

The excursion of cultivating an adoration for learning in youngsters is a profoundly remunerating one. It requires persistence, innovativeness, and a guarantee to developing a climate that values interest and investigation. By stressing the delight of learning, we plan kids for scholarly achievement, yet for a satisfying, energetic life loaded with ceaseless revelation. As we travel through this book, we'll investigate explicit procedures and bits of knowledge to motivate and sustain this long lasting excursion of learning.

This section sets the establishment for our investigation into the heap ways we can touch off the flash of interest in youngsters, guaranteeing it develops into a fire that lights their way over the course of life.

2

Chapter 2: Understanding Child Development

Exploring the Excursion of Development

Kid improvement is an excursion that starts upon entering the world and go on through adulthood. This way is set apart by huge achievements and stages, each described by extraordinary growth opportunities and open doors for development. Understanding these stages is urgent for anybody hoping to motivate an adoration for learning in youngsters, as it helps tailor ways to deal with suit their formative requirements.

Brief Outline of Youngster Improvement Stages

Youngster advancement can be comprehensively isolated into a few key stages:

1. Infancy (0-2 years): This stage is portrayed by fast actual development and the start of coordinated movements

improvement. Newborn children investigate their current circumstance basically through tangible encounters and development. Early interest is clear as they draw in with their environmental factors utilizing every one of the five detects.

2. Early Youth (2-6 years): During this period, youngsters foster language abilities, essential coordinated movements become more refined, and they begin to take part in more complicated play. Their reasoning is extremely concrete, and they learn best through direct encounters and collaborations. Interest is high, as they pose incalculable inquiries about their general surroundings.

3. Middle Youth (6-12 years): This stage sees the advancement of consistent reasoning, further developed memory and comprehension of intricate thoughts, yet inside substantial reality. Kids become more free and begin to frame their own groups of friends. Interest develops into more organized request, with an expanded limit with respect to learning and grasping the world's intricacies.

4. Adolescence (12-18 years): Youths foster the capacity to think conceptually and reason efficiently. Their interest might expand into additional theoretical areas, including character, connections, and their position on the planet. Learning turns out to be more independent, with peers assuming a critical part in impacting interests and inspirations.

How Interest Advances in Youngsters

Interest, the main thrust behind learning and investigation, advances fundamentally across these formative stages. In early stages, interest is about quick tactile encounters. As youngsters develop, their interest turns out to be more refined, advancing from straightforward investigations to complex inquiries regarding how the world functions.

In youth, interest appears through play and the steady "why" questions. By center youth, interest turns out to be more engaged, with kids looking to figure out rules, ideas, and the purposes for them. Puberty grows this interest further, integrating dynamic reasoning and investigation of complicated social and individual topics.

Perceiving Individual Contrasts in Learning

Every kid's excursion through these formative stages is exceptional. Contrasts in learning styles, interests, and speed of advancement are normal and ought to be embraced. A few kids might show an early interest in numbers and examples, while others are attracted to stories and language. Likewise, a few kids are normally more curious, while others might expect consolation to communicate their interest.

Perceiving and esteeming these distinctions is critical to cultivating a strong learning climate. It includes offering different learning open doors, obliging different learning styles, and empowering kids to seek after their inclinations. This customized approach regards every youngster's uniqueness as well as augments their commitment and happiness in learning.

Understanding kid advancement stages gives priceless experiences into how interest develops and how to best help every youngster's learning process. By perceiving the uniqueness of every youngster and fitting our way to deal with meet them where they are, we can rouse a long lasting adoration for learning. The following sections will dig further into commonsense methodologies for sustaining interest and advancing across these various stages, consistently with an eye toward perceiving and praising each youngster's singular way of revelation.

3

Chapter 3: The Role of Play in Learning

Uncovering the Force of Play

Play is many times seen as the language of kids, a widespread movement that rises above societies and ages. However, its job in learning and improvement is significantly more significant than simple amusement. Play is a basic vehicle for investigation, trial and error, and figuring out the world. It is through play that kids test speculations, take care of issues, and create essential abilities that serve them over the course of life.

The Instructive Worth of Play

Play isn't simply play. It is a significant business with regards to learning and improvement. The instructive worth of play lies in its capacity to cultivate mental, social, close to home, and actual development. Through play, kids foster language abilities, imagination, social intuition, and the capacity to tackle complex issues. Also, play animates brain associations in the mind, supporting the advancement of decisive reasoning and memory.

One of the vital parts of play is its job in upgrading inspiration and commitment. At the point when kids are participated in play, they are bound to face challenges, attempt new things, and persevere despite difficulties. This characteristic inspiration is vital for learning, as it drives kids to investigate further and learn all the more actually.

Various Kinds of Play and Their Advantages

Play comes in many structures, each with its own arrangement of advantages:

1. Physical Play (Running, Climbing, Moving): Supports coordinated movements advancement, coordination, and actual wellbeing. It additionally shows youngsters their bodies and the actual world.

2. Constructive Play (Working with Blocks, Drawing): Improves spatial thinking, innovativeness, and critical thinking abilities. It permits kids to try different things with materials and thoughts, fostering a pride and independence.

3. Pretend Assume (Pretending, Inventive Situations): Lifts language abilities, close to home getting it, and social capability. Through imagine play, kids investigate alternate points of view and foster compassion.

4. Games with Rules (Prepackaged games, Sports): Show kids rules, reasonableness, and participation. These games additionally foster vital reasoning and the capacity to concentrate and recall subtleties.

5. Social Play (Playing Along with Friends): Energizes relational abilities, cooperation, and grasping accepted practices. Social play is urgent for building connections and figuring out how to explore social circumstances.

Establishing Play Conditions That Support Learning

Establishing a climate that supports energetic learning includes something other than giving toys and materials. It requires a smart methodology that values have as a crucial impact of learning. Such conditions are wealthy in materials that animate imagination and investigation, offer places of refuge for risk-taking, and encourage social cooperation.

Here are a vital components to consider while establishing play conditions:

•Assortment and Adaptability: Give a scope of materials and exercises that take care of various interests and formative stages. Adaptable spaces that can be adjusted and reconsidered empower inventiveness and commitment.

•Availability: Guarantee that play materials and spaces are effectively open to youngsters, permitting them to freely investigate and draw in with them.

•Wellbeing: Establish a protected climate where youngsters have a solid sense of safety to investigate, examination, and face challenges.

•Consideration: Plan play spaces that are comprehensive and take special care of kids with different necessities and capacities.

•Nature: Consolidate regular components and outside play amazing open doors. Nature play upholds actual wellbeing, ecological mindfulness, and gives a rich tangible encounter.

The job of play in learning is obvious. It is through play that youngsters foster the abilities, information, and perspectives that set the establishment for long lasting learning. By perceiving the worth of play and establishing conditions that empower fun loving investigation, we support youngsters in their normal longing to learn, develop, and flourish. As we keep on investigating the manners by which we can motivate interest and learning, obviously have isn't recently an impact of learning; in numerous ways, it is its core.

4

Chapter 4: Cultivating a Growth Mindset

Embracing the Force of Yet

The idea of attitude, presented by analyst Hymn Dweck, has altered the manner in which we grasp learning, versatility, and achievement. At the core of Dweck's examination is a straightforward yet groundbreaking thought: the force of yet. This part investigates the qualification among development and fixed outlooks, offering methodologies to develop the previous in kids, subsequently outfitting them with the flexibility to defeat moves and the ability to gain from disappointment.

Prologue to Development versus Fixed Mentalities

A decent mentality is the conviction that capacities, insight, and gifts are fixed characteristics; we are brought into the world with a specific sum and it's a simple as that. Individuals with a decent outlook will generally keep away from difficulties, surrender effectively, see exertion as unbeneficial, and feel compromised by the outcome of others.

Conversely, a development mentality is the comprehension that capacities and insight can be created with exertion, learning, and industriousness. People with a development mentality embrace difficulties, persevere through hindrances, consider work to be the way to dominance, gain from analysis, and track down illustrations and motivation in the outcome of others.

Methodologies for Empowering a Development Mentality in Kids

1. Praise the Interaction, In addition to the Result: Spotlight on the work, methodology, and diligence kids put into their work, as opposed to simply adulating them for being shrewd or skilled. This builds up the worth of difficult work and the conviction that they can work on through exertion.

2. Use the Force of "Yet": When youngsters say they can't follow through with something, add a "yet" to their assertion. This basic word suggests that they are on an expectation to learn and adapt, and with time and exertion, they will actually want to accomplish their objectives.

3. Teach About the Mind: Teach kids on how the cerebrum develops further and shapes new associations when they master new things and practice abilities. Understanding this can persuade them to embrace learning and see knowledge as pliable.

4. Model a Development Mentality: Kids gain some significant experience from noticing grown-ups. Share your difficulties, what you're realizing, and the way in which you're continuing through challenges. Show them that battle and disappointment are regular pieces of the educational experience.

5. Encourage Gamble Requiring and Worth Exertion: Establish a protected climate where facing challenges and committing errors isn't simply acknowledged however celebrated as a

piece of learning. This urges youngsters to get out of their usual range of familiarity and attempt new things.

6. Use Useful Analysis: Input ought to be helpful and centered around how to move along. Urge youngsters to see analysis as important data that can assist them with developing.

Conquering Difficulties and Gaining from Disappointment

A development mentality is especially significant with regards to managing difficulties and disappointments. This is the way to assist youngsters with exploring these encounters:

1. Normalize Disappointment: Instruct kids that disappointment isn't an impression of their capacities yet rather a chance for development. Share accounts of effective individuals who fizzled and gained from their encounters.

2. Focus on Learning: After a misfortune, inquire, "What could we at any point gain from this?" Zeroing in on the learning perspective assists kids with considering inability to be a stage towards progress, not the finish of their excursion.

3. Encourage Tirelessness: Feature the significance of perseverance in accomplishing objectives. Urge youngsters to set little, reasonable objectives on the way to conquering a test, praising each forward-moving step.

4. Develop Critical thinking Abilities: Urge kids to consider various techniques they can use to handle an issue. This not just assists them with managing the ongoing test yet additionally outfits them with abilities for future hindrances.

Developing a development outlook in youngsters is a strong method for rousing an adoration for learning, strength even with difficulties, and the boldness to defy and develop from disappointments. It's tied in with instructing youngsters that their capacities are not fixed yet can be created through devotion and difficult work. This mentality establishes the groundwork for deep rooted learning and achievement, changing the manner in which kids view themselves and their true capacity in each attempt they embrace.

5

Chapter 5: Nurturing Curiosity through Questions

Encouraging the Curious Psyche

Interest is the driving force of scholarly accomplishment — the motivation drives us to continue getting the hang of, investigating, and developing. For kids, the world is a tremendous, baffling spot where everything merits addressing. By sustaining this intrinsic interest through the consolation of inquiries, we can fuel their longing to figure out the world and their place inside it. This part digs into procedures for empowering kids to clarify some pressing issues, methods for noting them successfully, and the significance of asking youngsters unassuming inquiries to animate their reasoning.

Empowering Youngsters to Seek clarification on some things

The capacity to pose inquiries is significant for mental turn of events and learning. Here are ways of empowering youngsters to embrace their regular interest:

1. Create a Place of refuge for Request: Clarify that all questions are esteemed and there are no "senseless" questions. A strong climate urges youngsters to voice their contemplations unafraid of judgment.
2. Model Interest: Kids advance as a visual cue. Show your own interest by posing inquiries resoundingly, investigating answers together, and exhibiting a certified revenue in finding new data.
3. Explore Together: Use books, nature strolls, and regular minutes as any open doors for investigation. Pose inquiries about what you see and urge kids to do likewise, directing them to notice and ponder their general surroundings.

Methods for Addressing Kids' Inquiries Actually
Answering kids' inquiries in a strong and viable way can additionally invigorate their interest and support further learning:

1. Listen Completely: Offer kids your full consideration when they get clarification on pressing issues. This shows that their interest is esteemed and their contemplations merit investigating.
2. Encourage Investigation: Rather than promptly giving a response, urge youngsters to contemplate potential responses themselves. Inquire, "What is your take?" This advances decisive reasoning and critical thinking abilities.
3. Provide Clear and Age-Fitting Responses: Designer your clarifications to the kid's age and level of understanding. Utilize straightforward language and substantial guides to assist them with embracing complex ideas.
4. Admit When You Don't Have any idea: It's alright to not have every one of the responses. Utilize these minutes as any

open doors to find answers together, showing that learning is a long lasting interaction.

The Craft of Posing Unassuming Inquiries

Inquiries without a right or wrong answer are incredible assets for invigorating idea and discussion. Dissimilar to yes-or-no inquiries, they urge kids to completely think basically and express their thoughts more. This is the way to successfully specialty and use them:

1. Encourage Elaboration: Pose inquiries that require in excess of a single word reply, for example, "What occurred straightaway?" or "For what reason do you believe that is?"
2. Foster Creative mind: Questions like "What might happen if...?" or "How might you tackle this issue?" energize innovative reasoning and critical thinking.
3. Promote Reflection: Questions, for example, "How did that cause you to feel?" or "What did you gain from this?" assist kids with considering their encounters and feelings.
4. Explore Conceivable outcomes: Urge kids to contemplate the future and expected results with questions like "What how about we find if we...?" This opens up a universe of potential outcomes and cultivates a feeling of experience in learning.

Questions are the keys that open the secrets of the world for youngsters. By empowering them to get clarification on pressing issues, noting them mindfully, and drawing in them with unconditional requests, we sustain their interest and prepare for a long period of learning and revelation. This approach improves their insight as well as fosters their decisive reasoning, imagination, and the ability to understand anyone on a deeper level, furnishing them with the devices they need to explore the intricacies of the world with certainty and interest.

6

Chapter 6: Learning in the Digital Age

Exploring the Computerized Learning Scene

The computerized age has changed the scene of training, offering uncommon admittance to data and better approaches for learning. Advanced apparatuses and assets can upgrade instructive encounters, making learning really captivating, available, and customized to individual necessities. In any case, exploring this new scene requires a smart way to deal with guarantee that computerized gaining supplements as opposed to reduces conventional, involved instructive strategies. This section investigates methodologies for adjusting advanced and actual learning devices, assessing the nature of computerized assets, and empowering kids to involve innovation in imaginative and basic ways.

Adjusting Advanced and Actual Learning Devices

A decent way to deal with computerized and actual learning perceives the worth of both and looks to coordinate them in manners that upgrade by and large learning:

1. Complementarity: Utilize computerized instruments to supplement actual growth opportunities. For instance, augmented reality can rejuvenate authentic occasions, adding profundity to course reading learning, while active trials in science can be enhanced with reproductions and online recordings.

2. Limit Setting: While computerized apparatuses offer many advantages, it means a lot to draw certain lines to forestall screen time from uprooting basic exercises like actual play, up close and personal social communications, and open air investigation.

3. Variety and Control: Give an assortment of opportunities for growth that draw in various faculties and learning styles. Blending computerized learning in with conventional techniques like perusing actual books, making craftsmanship, and participating in proactive tasks upholds a more comprehensive instructive experience.

Assessing the Nature of Computerized Learning Assets
With the immense range of computerized learning assets accessible, it is critical to guarantee quality:

1. Relevance and Precision: Pick assets that are applicable to the learning targets and verifiably exact. This frequently includes counseling surveys, teacher proposals, and legitimate instructive associations.

2. Engagement and Intelligence: Excellent computerized instruments ought to draw in understudies effectively, not latently. Search for assets that empower collaboration, critical thinking, and decisive reasoning.

3. Privacy and Wellbeing: Guarantee that advanced apparatuses and assets are ok for youngsters to use, with powerful security strategies safeguarding clients' data.

Empowering Imaginative and Basic Utilization of Innovation

Innovation isn't only for utilization; it very well may be a useful asset for creation and decisive reasoning:

1. Creative Ventures: Urge youngsters to utilize innovation to make, whether it's making a computerized story, forming music, planning a computer game, or building a site. This improves their specialized abilities as well as cultivates innovativeness and advancement.
2. Critical Reasoning: Help kids to basically assess the data they see as internet, recognizing valid sources and deception. Urge them to address and confirm data and to comprehend the predispositions that could exist in advanced content.
3. Collaborative Learning: Use innovation to work with cooperation, permitting kids to chip away at projects with peers, in any event, when truly separated. This can foster collaboration abilities and open them to different points of view.

Learning in the advanced age offers energizing chances to improve schooling and connect with youngsters in new and significant ways. By adjusting computerized and actual learning instruments, cautiously choosing excellent computerized assets, and empowering the innovative and basic utilization of innovation, we can furnish kids with a rich and differed instructive experience. This fair methodology sets them up not exclusively to succeed scholastically yet additionally to flourish in a computerized world, furnished with the abilities important to explore the intricacies of the data age with certainty and interest.

7

——

Chapter 7: The Power of Storytelling and Imagination

Opening Universes with Words

Narrating is an old work of art that has the ability to move audience members to new universes, inspire feelings, and give astuteness. With regards to youth picking up, narrating isn't simply a method for diversion; it is an imperative instrument for mental turn of events, the capacity to understand individuals on a profound level, and social holding. Through stories, youngsters figure out how to envision, identify, grasp the world according to different viewpoints. This part investigates how narrating can be utilized as a device for learning and holding, the job of inventive play in encouraging imagination, and the manners by which books and stories can move a long lasting affection for learning.

Narrating as an Instrument for Learning and Holding

1. Enhancing Language Abilities: Narrating acquaints youngsters with new jargon, etymological designs, and the rhythms of language, improving their relational abilities and language advancement.
2. Cultural and Moral Learning: Stories are a method for communicating social qualities and ethics, assisting kids with figuring out the intricacies of human way of behaving and morals.
3. Emotional Association: Sharing stories makes a novel connection among narrators and audience members, encouraging a conviction that all is good and having a place. This profound association is significant for a youngster's turn of events.

Empowering Inventive Play and Innovativeness

Inventive play, where kids make and carry on stories, is principal to mental and social turn of events:

1. Fostering Inventiveness: Through innovative play, kids explore different avenues regarding novel thoughts and situations, practicing their imaginative muscles and figuring out how to consider new ideas.
2. Developing Critical thinking Abilities: Innovative situations frequently include hindrances that should be survived, empowering kids to think basically and foster arrangements.
3. Understanding Oneself As well as other people: By taking on various jobs, kids investigate different viewpoints and feelings, upgrading their sympathy and comprehension of others.

Utilizing Books and Stories to Move Learning

Books and stories are priceless assets for moving interest and an affection for learning:

1. Broadening Skylines: Through stories, youngsters are acquainted with ideas, societies, and encounters past their nearby climate, widening how they might interpret the world.
2. Encouraging Investigation: Many kids' books are intended to ignite interest in nature, science, history, and craftsmanship, empowering further investigation and learning.
3. Inspiring Deep rooted Perusing: By developing an adoration for stories and perusing since the beginning, youngsters are bound to become energetic perusers, a propensity that supports advancing over the course of life.

The force of narrating and creative mind in learning couldn't possibly be more significant. By coordinating narrating into instructive works on, empowering inventive play, and involving books and stories as learning devices, we can open up a universe of opportunities for kids. Stories not just enhance youngsters' lives with amazement and fervor yet in addition outfit them with the devices they need to explore the intricacies of the world. Through the sorcery of narrating, we can move the cutting edge to dream, investigate, and find, encouraging a deep rooted love of discovering that rises above the limits of the study hall.

8

Chapter 8: Outdoor Learning and the Natural World

Reviving Training Through Nature

Open air learning and association with the normal world proposition priceless advantages to youngsters' actual wellbeing, mental prosperity, and instructive turn of events. Nature's study hall is vast, giving vast open doors to disclosure, interest, and active learning. This part investigates the diverse advantages of open air learning, presents thoughts for outside learning exercises, and examines ways of encouraging ecological mindfulness in youngsters, sustaining an age of educated and capable stewards of the planet.

Advantages of Open air Learning and Association with Nature

1. Enhanced Actual Wellbeing: Customary open air movement advances actual wellness, works on coordinated abilities, and

decreases the gamble of weight. The regular world supports dynamic play, which is significant for solid turn of events.

2. Improved Mental Prosperity: Time spent in nature has been displayed to decrease pressure, tension, and melancholy. The serenity of regular settings offers a rest from the tangible over-burden of metropolitan conditions and computerized screens.

3. Cognitive and Instructive Increases: Open air learning invigorates youngsters' interest and improves their observational abilities. It gives logical learning amazing open doors that make subjects like science, topography, and science more substantial and locking in.

4. Environmental Stewardship: Encountering nature firsthand cultivates a profound appreciation and regard for the climate, empowering kids to embrace feasible practices and become advocates for protection.

Thoughts for Open air Learning Exercises

Integrating open air learning into training can basic and award. Here are some action thoughts to begin:

1. Nature Strolls and Forager Chases: These exercises empower perception and investigation, assisting kids with finding out about nearby greenery. Consolidate undertakings like distinguishing tree species, noticing bug conduct, or gathering leaves of various shapes.

2. Gardening Tasks: Partaking in cultivating shows kids plant science, the significance of pollinators, and the nuts and bolts of food creation. It additionally imparts liability as they care for their plants.

3. Water Cycle and Climate Perception: Set up a downpour check, track weather conditions changes, and notice cloud

developments. These exercises offer pragmatic bits of knowledge into atmospheric conditions and the water cycle.

4. Outdoor Workmanship and Imagination: Utilize regular materials to make craftsmanship, empowering youngsters to see excellence in their environmental elements and express their imagination in remarkable ways.

5. Environmental Preservation Tasks: Take part in neighborhood tidy up endeavors, plant trees, or make living spaces for untamed life. These undertakings upgrade local area spaces and show important examples preservation.

Encouraging Natural Mindfulness

Developing a feeling of ecological obligation since the beginning is essential for the soundness of our planet. This is the way to impart natural mindfulness:

1. Lead As a visual cue: Exhibit harmless to the ecosystem practices like reusing, saving water, and decreasing waste. Youngsters learn best through perception and impersonation.

2. Discuss Ecological Issues: Acquaint youngsters with natural difficulties in age-suitable ways, zeroing in on how they can add to arrangements as opposed to feeling overpowered.

3. Encourage Backing: Backing kids in making a move on ecological causes they care about, whether it's composing letters, partaking in protection endeavors, or spreading mindfulness.

Open air learning and the normal world assume a basic part in youngsters' turn of events, offering an abundance of advantages that stretch out a long ways past scholarly accomplishment. By drawing in youngsters in outside learning exercises and cultivating an association with nature, we outfit them with the information, abilities, and enthusiasm expected to have sound existences and safeguard the planet for people in the future. As teachers, guardians, and watchmen, it's our obligation to make the way for nature's study hall, welcoming kids to investigate, find, and learn in nature.

9

Chapter 9: The Importance of Emotional Intelligence

Developing Hearts and Brains

The ability to appreciate individuals on a profound level (EI) is as basic to kids' improvement as their scholarly development. It incorporates the capacity to comprehend and deal with one's own feelings, understand others, and explore social intricacies successfully. This section highlights the meaning of encouraging ability to appreciate people on a profound level in kids, featuring its effect on understanding and dealing with feelings, compassion and participation, and the essential job of close to home flexibility in learning and by and large prosperity.

Understanding and Dealing with Feelings

1. Self-mindfulness: Helping youngsters to perceive and name their feelings is the most important phase in ability to

understand anyone on a deeper level. Exercises like inclination graphs or diaries can assist kids with articulating their sentiments.

2. Self-guideline: When kids comprehend their feelings, the following stage is figuring out how to oversee them. Methods like profound breathing, counting, or enjoying some time off can engage kids to productively deal major areas of strength for with.

3. Emotion Articulation: Youngsters ought to have a real sense of reassurance communicating their feelings. Empowering open correspondence and giving a strong climate where kids can discuss their thoughts unafraid of judgment is vital.

Compassion, Collaboration, and Social Learning

1. Developing Compassion: Sympathy is the capacity to comprehend and discuss the thoughts of another. Pretending, narrating, and examining different situations can assist youngsters with imagining others' perspective, cultivating a more profound comprehension of others' viewpoints.

2. Promoting Collaboration: Helpful games and gathering ventures can show kids how to cooperate, share, and arrange. Figuring out how to see things from numerous perspectives upgrades critical thinking abilities and social congruity.

3. Enhancing Interactive abilities: The capacity to appreciate individuals on a deeper level is critical to creating solid interactive abilities. Exercises that include cooperation, correspondence, and understanding meaningful gestures can work on kids' communications and associations with others.

Close to home Versatility and Its Job in Learning

1. Building Versatility: Close to home strength is the capacity to return from difficulties or difficulties. Instructing kids that disappointment is a piece of learning and development is fundamental for creating flexibility.
2. Coping Procedures: Furnish youngsters with systems to adapt to dissatisfaction, disappointment, and disappointment. Examining previous encounters and conceptualizing arrangements can assist youngsters with figuring out how to successfully explore future difficulties more.
3. Positive Mentality: Empowering an inspirational perspective and appreciation can assist youngsters with keeping up with profound equilibrium and versatility. Practices, for example, appreciation diaries or sharing positive encounters can support good faith and constancy.

The capacity to understand anyone on a profound level is primary to youngsters' progress in school and life. By getting it and dealing with their feelings, creating compassion, and figuring out how to help out others, youngsters can explore the intricacies of social associations and difficulties with certainty. Besides, by developing profound versatility, youngsters are more ready to confront misfortunes and keep learning with a positive and development situated outlook. In cultivating the capacity to understand people on a profound level, we furnish youngsters with scholarly abilities as well as with the close to home devices essential for a satisfying and healthy lifestyle.

10

Chapter 10: Involving Parents and Caregivers

Engaging the Main Instructors

Guardians and parental figures assume an essential part in a kid's schooling. Their contribution can essentially upgrade the opportunity for growth, giving a strong groundwork to scholarly achievement and self-improvement. This part dives into the essential job grown-ups play in supporting youngsters' learning, presents pragmatic thoughts for instructive exercises at home, and examines ways of building an energetic learning local area that reaches out past the study hall.

The Job of Grown-ups in Supporting Youngsters' Learning

1. Creating a Strong Climate: A home climate that qualities and empowers learning is key. This incorporates having books and instructive materials promptly accessible, saving a tranquil and agreeable space for study, and laying out schedules that focus on learning exercises.

2. Active Commitment: Guardians and parental figures ought to effectively take part in their kid's schooling by remaining informed about their advancement, going to class gatherings, and discussing consistently with educators. Showing interest in their learning process conveys its significance and worth.

3. Encouragement and Backing: Giving consolation and backing, particularly when kids face scholarly difficulties, is critical. Praising endeavors and progress, as opposed to simply accomplishments, cultivates a development outlook and versatility.

Thoughts for Instructive Exercises at Home

Taking part in instructive exercises at home can support school learning and animate interest. Here are a few thoughts:

1. Reading Together: Perusing books together further develops proficiency abilities as well as upgrades profound holding. Examining the accounts and characters can additionally foster appreciation and decisive reasoning abilities.

2. Practical Numerical Exercises: Integrate math into regular exercises, like cooking (estimating fixings), shopping (computing expenses), or playing tabletop games that include counting and system.

3. Science Tests: Straightforward investigations utilizing family things can demystify science ideas and empower request based learning. For instance, investigating the properties of water, developing plants, or concentrating on the periods of the moon.

4. Art and Imagination: Empower inventive articulation through drawing, painting, music, and artworks. These exercises cultivate creative mind, fine coordinated abilities, and profound articulation.

5. Exploring Nature: Standard trips to parks, nature saves, or the lawn can ignite interest in science, biology, and ecological stewardship.

Building a Learning People group

Making a strong organization of guardians, parental figures, educators, and local area individuals can intensify the advantages of locally situated learning:

1. Parent Gatherings: Joining or framing guardian gatherings can give a stage to sharing assets, encounters, and exhortation. These gatherings can put together studios, talks, or gathering exercises that benefit the kids and the local area.
2. Community Assets: Libraries, exhibition halls, public venues, and nearby associations frequently offer instructive projects, clubs, and occasions that can enhance a youngster's opportunity for growth.
3. Collaboration with Schools: Building areas of strength for a with schools empowers guardians and parental figures to adjust home learning exercises to the educational plan and school goals. Taking part in school occasions and volunteer open doors further fortifies this association.

Including guardians and parental figures in the instructive excursion is critical for youngsters' turn of events and achievement. By establishing a steady learning climate at home, participating in improving instructive exercises, and encouraging a cooperative learning local area, grown-ups can essentially influence their kids' adoration for learning, scholarly accomplishments, and by and large prosperity. Together, guardians, parental figures, and instructors can develop a biological system that supports inquisitive, certain, and deep rooted students.

11

Chapter 11: Overcoming Obstacles to Learning

Outlining the Way Through Difficulties

Each kid's learning process incorporates its portion of impediments. These difficulties can go from hardships understanding specific ideas to physical, profound, or ecological elements that effect learning. Distinguishing and tending to these obstructions is critical for guaranteeing that all kids have the chance to succeed and flourish scholastically. This part investigates techniques for beating impediments to getting the hang of, supporting youngsters with different advancing necessities, and the significance of encouraging constancy and versatility.

Recognizing and Tending to Learning Obstructions

1. Early ID: Perceiving indications of learning challenges almost immediately is basic. This can remember noticing changes for conduct, disappointment with explicit errands, or an unexpected drop in scholastic execution.

2. Seek Expert Guidance: Assuming learning hindrances are thought, looking for assessments from instructive clinicians or experts can give clearness and bearing. These experts can recognize explicit learning problems, mental difficulties, or intense subject matters influencing learning.
3. Tailored Methodologies: When learning obstructions are recognized, creating customized learning plans that take care of the kid's particular necessities can have a massive effect. This could include elective showing strategies, one-on-one mentoring, or the utilization of assistive innovation.

Supporting Kids with Various Advancing Necessities

1. Inclusive Instruction: Schools and homerooms ought to take a stab at inclusivity, where offspring of all capacities and learning styles are invited, esteemed, and upheld. This incorporates open materials, educational program transformations, and a steady homeroom climate.
2. Parent and Guardian Contribution: Guardians and parental figures assume a crucial part in supporting their kids' advancing at home. This can include working intimately with instructors, finishing suggested exercises or treatments, and giving reliable consolation and understanding.
3. Building on Qualities: Each kid has novel qualities and interests. Zeroing in on these areas can support certainty and commitment, filling in as an establishment for handling additional difficult subjects or abilities.

The Job of Constancy and Flexibility

1. Cultivating a Development Mentality: Urge youngsters to consider difficulties to be valuable open doors for

development. Instruct them that work and tirelessness can prompt improvement and achievement, even notwithstanding challenges.

2. Adaptability: Helping kids to be versatile even with difficulties is similarly significant. This incorporates assisting them with figuring out how to change their procedures, look for help when required, and stay open to attempting new methodologies.

3. Celebrating Exertion and Flexibility: Perceive and celebrate accomplishments as well as the work, progress, and strength kids show in conquering hindrances. This builds up the worth of tirelessness and the faith in their capacity to conquer difficulties.

Conquering deterrents to learning is an excursion that requires persistence, understanding, and custom-made help. By recognizing learning hindrances early, offering designated help, and cultivating a culture of constancy and versatility, we can enable all youngsters to effectively explore difficulties. This supports their scholarly accomplishments as well as constructs fundamental abilities that will work well for them past the study hall. In doing as such, we confirm the conviction that each youngster can possibly learn and develop, regardless of the impediments they might confront.

12

Chapter 12: Inspiring Examples and Case Studies

Observing Victories in Training

Across the globe, innumerable students, instructors, and networks are thinking outside the box, beating difficulties, and spearheading imaginative ways to deal with training. Their accounts act as signals of motivation, delineating the groundbreaking force of enthusiasm, imagination, and versatility in the learning venture. This section features rousing models and contextual investigations that exhibit pivotal learning conditions, novel instructive methodologies, and the unimaginable accomplishments of people focused on schooling.

Accounts of Rousing Students and Teachers

1. Malala Yousafzai's Battle for Training: Malala's gallant support for young ladies' schooling even with outrageous difficulty

has propelled millions around the world. Her story highlights the force of instruction to switch lives and the significance of waiting around for the option to learn.

2. The Creative Teacher from Finland: Pasi Sahlberg, a Finnish instructor and researcher, has been instrumental in molding Finland's eminent schooling system, which underscores value, prosperity, and a toning it down would be ideal methodology. His work features the effect of fundamental change in training.

3. Jaime Escalante's Math Upset: The momentous story of Jaime Escalante, a Bolivian teacher who changed a striving ghetto secondary school in East Los Angeles by rousing his understudies to make phenomenal progress in analytics, exhibits the significant impact of exclusive standards and unfaltering faith in understudies' true capacity.

Inventive Learning Conditions and Approaches

1. Montessori Schools: The Montessori technique, created by Dr. Maria Montessori, underscores independent movement, involved learning, and cooperative play. Montessori schools all over the planet keep on rousing through their obligation to supporting free, certain students.

2. Outdoor Schools in Scandinavia: In nations like Denmark and Sweden, woods schools and open air learning are vital to youth training. These schools feature the advantages of nature-based instruction, encouraging actual wellbeing, inventiveness, and ecological stewardship.

3. STEAM Methodologies in South Korea: South Korea's combination of Science, Innovation, Designing, Artistic expression, and Arithmetic (STEAM) into schooling features the significance of interdisciplinary learning and imagination in

getting ready understudies for the intricacies of the cutting edge world.

Illustrations from Around the World

1. Singapore's Attention on Decisive Reasoning: Singapore's school system is famous for its accentuation on decisive reasoning and critical thinking abilities. By incorporating true applications into the educational program, Singapore shows the way that instruction can be both thorough and significant.
2. New Zealand's Fuse of Native Viewpoints: New Zealand's schooling system has made progress in integrating Maori culture and points of view into the educational plan, offering examples on the worth of social variety and consideration in training.
3. Bhutan's Accentuation on Satisfaction: Bhutan's interesting spotlight on Gross Public Joy over GDP reaches out to its school system, which focuses on the prosperity and joy of understudies. This approach gives significant bits of knowledge into the job of profound and social learning in training.

The rousing models and contextual analyses introduced in this part mirror the different manners by which training can be drawn closer and the significant effect it can have on people and social orders. These accounts celebrate accomplishments as well as act as strong tokens of the expected that exists in each student and teacher. By drawing illustrations from creative practices and the mental fortitude of the people who have changed training in their specific circumstances, we can keep on pushing the limits of what is conceivable in realizing conditions around the world.

13

Chapter 13: Resources and Further Reading

Engaging Consistent Development

The excursion of realizing, whether it's tied in with sustaining interest in kids, embracing imaginative showing techniques, or cultivating an adoration for training, is progressing. This section incorporates an arranged rundown of assets, including books, sites, and expert associations, focused on instructors, guardians, and anybody focused on the instructive excursion. Furthermore, it features online networks that interface similar people to share bits of knowledge, difficulties, and victories. These assets are venturing stones for the people who wish to dive further into the domains of schooling, youngster improvement, and deep rooted learning.

Suggested Books, Sites, and Different Assets

1. Books:

    o"Mindset: The New Brain research of Accomplishment" via Tune S. Dweck investigates the idea of development mentality and its effect on different parts of life, including instruction.

o"How Youngsters Learn" by John Holt gives bits of knowledge into the regular educational experiences of kids and studies conventional tutoring techniques.

o"The Spongy Brain" by Maria Montessori offers an inside and out check out at the Montessori technique and its philosophical underpinnings on youngster improvement and instruction.

2. Websites:

oEdutopia (edutopia.org): Offers an abundance of assets on inventive schooling works on, including articles, recordings, and techniques for K-12 instructors.

oKhan Institute (khanacademy.org): Gives free internet based seminars on a great many subjects for students, everything being equal, supporting customized instruction ways.

oTED-Ed (ed.ted.com): Elements instructive recordings on different points that flash interest and advance advancing past the study hall.

3. Other Assets:

oNational Geographic Children and BBC Bitesize offer connecting with content and exercises intended to make learning fun and open for youngsters.

oDuolingo, a language learning application, gamifies the method involved with learning new dialects, making it pleasant for students, everything being equal.

Proficient Associations and Online People group

1. Professional Associations:

oThe Public Instruction Affiliation (NEA) and the Global Proficiency Affiliation (ILA) give assets and backing to instructors, including proficient turn of events and strategy support.

oThe Relationship for Management and Educational plan Improvement (ASCD) offers instructive authority assets, including books, gatherings, and online courses.

2. Online People group:

oReddit Instruction (r/training) and Instructor's Corner are gatherings where teachers share assets, homeroom methodologies, and backing.

oParenting and instructive subreddits, like r/Nurturing and r/Self-teach, offer spaces for guardians to look for guidance, share encounters, and track down instructive assets.

Proceeding with the Excursion of Learning

The quest for information and the mission to motivate learning in others is a long lasting excursion. By drawing in with the assets and networks referenced in this part, teachers, guardians, and students can track down help, motivation, and a feeling of kinship. The way of schooling is always advancing, with new speculations, systems, and innovations arising continually. Remaining educated and associated is critical to exploring these progressions and proceeding to motivate and be roused by the delight of learning.

As this book closes, recall that each step taken to enhance the instructive encounters of youngsters is a stage toward a more brilliant, more inquisitive, and proficient world. Allow these assets to be your aide as you progress forward with this compensating way.

14

Chapter 14: Conclusion

An Excursion of Disclosure and Development

As we arrive at the finish of this investigation into "The Delight of Picking up: Motivating Interest in Kids," we ponder the excursion we've left upon together. From understanding the formative phases of kids to embracing the computerized time of learning, every part has added to a thorough embroidery showing how we can support and move a significant love of learning in youngsters. This finishing up section tries to sum up the vital subjects of the book, repeat the significance of encouraging interest, and express last impressions on the persevering through effect of schooling that is established in investigation and marvel.

Summing up the Critical Topics of the Book

This book has crossed a wide cluster of points, every integral to the core of instructive way of thinking and practice:

•The basic significance of understanding kid advancement to tailor growth opportunities that meet youngsters at their place of need.

•The pivotal job of play in getting the hang of, offering kids a dynamic and intuitive stage to investigate, question, and find.

•The meaning of developing a development outlook, which enables kids to see difficulties as any open doors for development instead of unfavorable obstructions.

•The force of inquiries to drive request, understanding, and a more profound association with our general surroundings.

•The groundbreaking capability of innovation when offset with customary learning modalities, improving instructive encounters and availability.

•The persevering through benefit of narrating and creative mind in encouraging imagination, sympathy, and a more profound comprehension of different encounters and societies.

•The advantages of open air learning and its job in advancing natural stewardship, actual wellbeing, and a feeling of miracle.

•The basic significance of the ability to appreciate people on a profound level in schooling, outfitting kids with the abilities to successfully explore their feelings and social communications.

•The effect of parental and guardian contribution in supporting learning outside the homeroom and building a steady instructive local area.

•Techniques for conquering hindrances to picking up, guaranteeing each kid has the chance to succeed no matter what the difficulties they face.

•Moving models and contextual investigations that feature inventive ways to deal with training and the momentous accomplishments of students and teachers all over the planet.

Empowering Perusers to Cultivate an Affection for Learning

As perusers, you are furnished with bits of knowledge, systems, and motivations to have a substantial effect in the existences of kids. The development of an adoration for learning is maybe the most significant gift we can propose to the more youthful age — a gift that opens potential, opens ways to boundless conceivable outcomes, and enhances lives with information, understanding, and euphoria.

Last Considerations on the Effect of Moving Interest in Kids

Motivating interest in youngsters isn't only an instructive objective; it is a significant interest from here on out. Inquisitive personalities question, investigate, advance, and eventually, drive mankind forward. By encouraging an affection for learning, we not just upgrade the individual and scholastic existences of individual youngsters yet additionally add to the improvement of smart, compassionate, and educated residents regarding the world.

As this book closes, let it mark not the end but rather the start of a restored obligation to sustaining the vast interest inside every kid. In doing as such, we light a flash that can enlighten ways, change lives, and light up the future — each inquisitive psyche in turn.